About The Trod

Play Date

Rite to lament precious experiences
Rite to materialize splendor
        in thoughts imagination
Rite as there's sweet sweet joy
        down in the heart
Rite for innocent playdates with
        words and create also teach and inspire
Rite just in case report's page gets torn
        for repeat and report are pages in an
        important book

Listen so you remember to remember
        consider to consider
Listen for notes guiding through dimensions
        over hills and down in valleys
Listen to explore that perfect place of thrill
Listen making time for both love and enjoy

www.ingramcontent.com/pod-product-compliance
Lightning Source LLC
Chambersburg PA
CBHW060921140726

47996CB00001B/330

About The Trod

Moving around plateaus
Up in the mountains

Poems by DreamKeypr

I.R.I.E. SUITE

CONTENTS

Acknowledging

Combing through vocabulary sieving out words to find sight. A perfect rhythm to make sound come forth right. Gratitude overwhelms to an overflow from the outpour of love and patience that was shown. None of these pages would be real with words that feel had there not been living writing prompts that breathe.

Give thanks to Jah the master of the universe for

all things, his blessings beyond visions, my wildest hopes, dreams or aspirations. Thankful for the presence of angels with wings of support, guidance, protection, tolerance and correction.

My heart drums in thanksgiving reverberating with love for my children, my family and circle of friends for enveloping me with commitment. To reach even higher to soar.

For my invisible love that captivated my heart and sweetened my soul. Holding me close patiently helping me share my voice. Please know this heart is smothered with appreciation and delights in feelings running wild for you.

The eye of perception sees reality.
What it sees, is what it is.

Preface

For Interested Eyes

A very many that helped make this all true
You included too. That's right I said you!
For giving lyrics and verses your precious time of day.
In love and hope that with you a few of them will stay.
I can't voice enough to thank you too much
for investing time to read my headspace as it bleeds.
Give thanks to the creator for gifting the words.
Sending angelic help that poured in streams.
That toiled to inspire
worked tirelessly using means.
Words can't say begin to capture or tell
this crescendo of gratitude within me that dwells.

About The Trod
Along hillsides
moving around plateaus

———————————

1

LOVELY

APERTURE

Evry hoe ave 'im tick a bush.

ON THE EARS: For every hoe there's a stick in the bush.

FOR THE HEART: Everyone can find love somewhere.

Sign On A Sill
    No neon lights
    Colors lace or frill
    Not propped up
    Pinned nor posted
    No flashing lights
    Sounding board
    Alarms bells or whistles

    Word pair
    To one lines drawn
    Grand meaning
    Eloquence they spell
    Grandeur of inspiration
    Speech can't expel

    Flying through thickets
    Against strong breeze
    Down in valleys
    High against
    Vast mountainous skies

To feel to move
To love to glow
To tell to show
All this
From a simple
Sign standing sill
Don't wish
Do!

Lovely Play
When I dive in myself
It's my movie
With story that never ends
Thing is though—
Don't see my cast
I see you, the only part
A crave to consume

Creative plot diagram
Exposition of two
Rising action magnificent view
A climax so heavenly
Action that's falling to start anew
I see you, so I hit pause and then play

When I dive in my head
It's treasured time
I have you all to myself
A frolic with my thoughts
A body thrill
Limbs bursting to form an arch
Faint deep breaths filling contours
And curves in my head
No empty spaces
For anything instead
I see you, so I hit pause and then play

When I dive into my heart
It's no longer brainwork
But an outright action
A dance with no care
For what moves or
In what order— whatsoever
As long as they're with you
They're perfect with rhythm and grace
I see you, so I hit pause and then play

When I dive into my dreams
It's a memory of love
From a lifetime ago
I know it so well
I taste your scent and catch your touch
I see you, so I hit pause and then play

Your caress a silken kiss that hits my lips
As the sun meets the base of the sky
Or tickles that fall as gentle as dusk
I see just you, savoring fountain of sacral
When day rests at night and
Does it again and again
So it repeats and repeats
I see you, so I hit pause and then play

When I dive into my soul
Entranced by your command, no utterance
Nor words planned
Its fingers stretched making velvety smooth
Water shapes swirling on crevices and corners
Rise and dips a stream of tender love welts
Allowing— I concede, making my insides melt
I see you, so I hit pause and then play

Wanna hear a secret
No a promise—this is real, true
For us this is nothing that's new
A reincarnated love through and through
I'm gonna recline
All the way front and center into my head
Holding you their cause

You are my person
That drenches and swallows
My soul—
No wish to control
Its forwards Eva backwards Neva
So I will pause and play and play and pause
Till never ends always and forever
So we can love another mortal lifespan
Again and again, again

As Liking It
All worlds a stage
All men women merely players
Liking it, liking it a lot!

Liking absolute without any blunder
Liking not knowing and all in wonder
Chanting your name driving insane
When came forth from the brain
Caught site from live feed
Watched wondered and believed
Even pondered if succeed

Mystic not faked
Holding pendulous and in place
Reservations any hesitations
Dissolving with no trace
Wanting just a little taste
A sweet embrace
As lips will allow
Wonderings
Could be one that heart will endow?

Liking that charm is unreal
A captivating feel
That makes sparkle and twinkle
Dissolving denial soothing wrinkles
Mind trips be taking
Fabulous fantasies mixing making
Pleasured purple bruised from bliss
To dismiss desire unreservedly amiss!

Liking willingness and ease
With expertise that are keys
To lifting higher and higher
Elevated lighter lighter—
Liking and can't ignore
Finding without looking
Treasure in view
Unwrapping full measure
Possible concept of two

Liking imperial teachings unfold
To pass on not withhold
Humbly walking in stride
With the righteous
Spreading love contagiously
Like a virus

Mind gladly paying ransom
To sagacity and wisdom
Freeing thoughts evoked
To reality and then some
Intently falling admits
Savoring details bit by bit
No need for guessing
Games need quit!
For
It's as liking it!

Thank You

    Such as this can't be undone
    The highest paved way no pun
    Tickles from delight surely have begun
    Weaving interest in motion already been spun

    Holding thoughts here captive
    Unknowing with charming embrace
    Wanted perhaps vital headspace
    Amidst noise from trauma encased
    Positive lovely thoughts
    With certainty a keeper
    Feelings like this nudge you deeper

    Such as this can't be undone
    The highest paved way no pun
    Tickles from delight surely have begun
    Weaving interest in motion already been spun

    Turning aside
    That excites sent to hide
    Can no way be
    Not a possibility—
    Whys and wherefores?
    Sugared way too much
    Perfectly fitting
    Sweet spot so much

Such as this can't be undone
The highest paved way no pun
Tickles from delight surely have begun
Weaving interest in motion already been spun

Thank you for being just you
Joy speaks for meeting you
Pure joy with smiles random thoughts of you
Full joy for then, next when present with you

Sweet Rose

Accolades with graceful
Gratitude for sweet Rose!
Purifying most precious
Inner part of bosom

For encouraging blossoms of
Peace calm and comfort
For creating channels
From deep within
To flow freely to-and-fro
For balancing physical
Releasing impurities
Hastening securities

For all fullness of wisdom
In life's divine design
With divine plan
For knowledge that
Walking without at best
Must end as simple sweet distaste
Always compelling
A rise in Love Love Love!

For gift without condition
Universal motherly
For platonic romantic
All in perfect love
For stirred in and sweetened
With loving care and loving kindness
Heartfelt appreciation
For sweet rose quartz

Love Glitch

Gliding on bliss is breathtaking
Gliding is heavenly with joy sweet joy
Joy the foundation for intimate sparks
Joy that scorched passionate desire
Desire can torture, torment the soul
Desire charms enchanting treasures

Treasures as blessings beyond measure
Treasures baked on plenty good things
Things as thoughts ponder as gifts
Things that delight evolve from waves of trust
Trust and kindness, ingredients to win
Trust is releasing, never coercing within

Within look deeply, there stashed is a vault
Within rays beaming with doting devotion
Devotion of wrapped persistence echoing more
Devotion whispering fiercely, complemented by love
Love an explanation, cautious, timid to respond
Love always some ACTION! Never a reaction

Reaction promises captivity with judgment and fears
Reaction mutes the laughter of love
Love radiates light, sincere magical beauty
Love dances faultless with secure unbothered freedom
Freedom to express
Freedom to cover

Cover together love, tuck roll
Cover game, hide with thrill to seek
Seek with motive on motivation
Seek intent, wondrous happiness
Happiness forms from self to self
Happiness controls first head and then heart

Heart, overflow no boundaries can contain
Heart, natural equanimity balanced with love
Love given and received
Love not given for a receipt
Receipt no part in this at all
Receipt speaks gratitude only for gifts

Gifts one symbol a probability of feeling
Gifts may give a meaningful pleasured smile
Smile radiantly, break out in sparkle
Smile unapologetically, proclaim the feel of it
It is no worries it doesn't take over
It is virtuous and true for self for you

You exceed the impossible permeating probable
You imagine creative expectations to create
Create sensations with cause of wonder
Create with euphoric joy
Joy, there's joy down in my heart
Joy, essential for divine unearthly love
Love is the answer
Heart of absolute cosmic love

A-new Song

Lioness
Willing cautious ready and steady
Conscious sufficient stable real
And able— to full joy a new view

She is
Poised, a bright new beginning
Forwards to ever
All with splendor abundance to unfold
Truly with no effort or words told—
Lion charmed the heart straight through
To every part from the very start
Radical in position, wired for him
Inarguably incontestably
Complete guiltless and painless
Kindly perfectly effortless solely his
Congo bongo Empress

Her Presence

Thirty and one
They march to exit
In heightened anticipation
For her presence
For she's a lady
With grace that's next to none

Awestruck, eyes frozen
Fixed in perfect gaze
Her beauty casts
Holding, set in place

As enters
Promising treasures
Gems they seek
Attempts to clutch
Enchanted phenomenon
Pouring purity and peace

Festival that celebrates
Grand awakening
That clears channel enlivening!
With honor it acclaims
Diamond delight eruption
Loving surge object affection

Lovely Rider

Smooth rider real feeler
All in all alluring
A pull on you from only them
Mystic rider private pleasure
Down to core compelling
Eyes on you for none but them

Unaware grips restraint no fear
Inhibitions freely care to share
For just one that came through
Only one the main view
From phantom nothing
Not one solitary stroke
Slightest touch it's no joke
Not one word a sound or a poke

A move
That makes her dance
To bust a move getting in the groove
When given the chance
A smile
That makes her face twitch
Forms lips like a glitch
Then just as quick
Sides come down in a frown

Motions
That gives her inspiration
To stand up and fight
Only spitting verses for what's right
Dreams creative sway
Disguised special way
Responding moves made
Obey cosmic orders
Descending heavenly quarters

The Meeting

Waiting with tiny waves crashing
Walking as thoughts compete in race
He waits, she walks
Eyes meet, smiles greet
Each with a nervous face

Linking to hold a reason
Planned guided by the king up high
Paired to fit that truly hits
New lively chatter can't deny

Enjoying tall all she sees
But hides so as not to call notice
Then a heavy tongue other becomes
A disappearing ghost lotus

She ponders how precocious
She can't forget nor jade
Impression that was made
Pendulous yet held in place

Same So

Heartfelt inside, unfaltering outside
Spans near, up close and far, vast wide
Overflows boundaries, that verb
Always an action none wise a reaction
Provides no judgment, can make you so nervous
Feeling more than yesterday
But not as much as tomorrow
Same So

Permeates smiles, giggles even laughter
Crescendo of feelings divine
Stick with it ride or die kinda thing
Feeling pleasured purple in fact
Filling up and pouring out
Never to dominate another
Always allowing freedom
Shows delicacy in a delicate way
Same so

Captivating yet releasing
Intoxicating reckless stirred and shaken
Yielding muted speech
Sees sense when there is nonsense
Propelled by heartbeats and headaches
A rhythm, twin gyrations
On occasion slow, steady
Then some rapid fierce—
Oh dear!
Same so

No fear with expression
A simple touch uplifts
Movement without conditions
Unconditionally
Soul to Soul connections
Fleeting nowhere in sight
Scorched by desire, quenched with passion
Random thoughts creating sparkle
Souvenirs of words
Moments, all treasured
Waiting with bated breath
For what's next
Same so

Go For It
A tickle that exhilarates
It fits comfortable can't obliterate
Never mind no sounding board
still worthy from emotions stored
A wish for reach grasp of trust
enduring preparing to adjust to stretch
Plummet oneself in discomfort robust
Careful stumble of strokes for
One LOVEly sketch

Lifetime

Starting out as strangers
Really close yet oh so far
Without any warning
Fate brings right on par
Looking but not looking
So as not to deceive
Leaving first encounter
Wanting more to conceive

Can plainly see it
Known what's felt from it
Unsure what to make of it
No questions shall ask of it

Fondness feeling friendship
Words that float to mind
Playful timed so sweetly
Interactions come to life
Blissful heavenly excitement
Engulfing trails to ascend
Promising always and forever
Guidance recommends

Can plainly see it
Known what's felt from it
Completely giving into it
No questions shall ask of it

Lives dance together
Starting steps this new role
And with a tiny symbol
Pouring heart love
Outpouring soul
Forever's no way sufficient
Enough to ever spend
This known for sure is true
Can never ever contend
Finding the love of a lifetime
That doesn't ever end

Can plainly see it
Totally committed to it
Still disbelief questions experiencing it
With certainty knowing this is it!
This love of a lifetime

On Full
     He takes the breath
     He's the ex-hale
     As a plant to help grow
     He would be sustenance
     To thrive making glow glow
     On full from that man
     Wanting it all so much

     Whispering to the atmosphere
     Trusting connects out there
     Words do no justice
     Describe what's happening here
     On full from that man
     Moved in permanently
     Made his bed in the head

     Within these feelings
     Deep inside so severe
     Mounting effects completely sincere
     Yelling on full from that man
     One exploding body trap
     Waiting to happen

Eagerly walking in sweet
Anticipation to be with him
Placidly floating
Regal reflections all about him
On full from that man
Anticipation of experiencing
Flight of fantasies into existence

Fastened
Without a desire to be free
Each encounter a divine melody
Snatching the soul
Holding onto tenderly
Juggling with it timeless
Leaving longing and helpless
Without any control
On full, full— from that man

When spirits collide
Join and enter-twine
Sweet energy perfect sublime
On full from that man
Together
creating a delightful disaster

2

TURNS

Your Right
    Might
    It tells all
    Of treasures
    Pleased to come right in
    Heavenly, superb celestial energy
    Clarity with spiritual contemplation

    Majestic mirror divine reflection
    Pinnacle of sight, added benefits
    Of sixth sense, so good sense
    Enticing shimmering
    Pulling deeper, farther
    Grander

U A Gem
Shielding temple of us
Builds boosts blood bones breath in bounty
Gene line that mends

Inside Out

Suppose the world was inside out
The sky would be the ground
Stars would switch places with people
The world would be upside down

Suppose the world was inside out
Then inner parts from all of us
Would be out on display
Then people would consider to
Consider what they have mind over
Cause their life would be an open book
Cause it would be inside out

Suppose, just suppose
The world was inside out
Then with attitudes any side
Would be the right side
Never, never a wrong side

Then truth would overtake lies
And win, win the chase every time
Cause lies couldn't outrun or hide
Cause it would be inside out

Suppose, let's juxtapose
The world was inside out
Then mind games would be
Pointless no winner no loser

No beggars not, not being choosers
Then hate would dissipate
Leaving only love
Cause the heart would be visible
Clear and free, free in view of all to see
Cause it would be inside out

So can we move as though?
All insides throughout
Opened wide and are showing out!

That Rose

Passionate in rose
You evoke a loving thread
Lasting gem a ruby pose

See Saw

    Take my hand, journey with me
    This orange hue that guides, come see
    See Saw Carnelian Law
    See, acceptance whatever will come
    See, welcome life's possibilities
    All to become
    See, positivity the sole force
    That hums
    See, joy pleasure family together
    Love the total sum.

    See Saw Carnelian Law
    Johnny shall have a new mantra
    He shall be very happy each day
    Cause he will follow the Tantra.

    See Saw Carnelian Law
    Saw, past fears of death, remove!
    No untruths nothing is lost
    Or gone in truth
    Saw, uncertainty delay and indecision
    Transmute!

Deciding with certainty
Just as in youth.
Saw, reluctance to modify
Or alter, transform!
Change will come so
Change must happen!

See Saw Carnelian Law
Johnny shall have a new mantra
He shall be very happy each day
Cause he will follow the Tantra.

Cancel, erase all thoughts
For preview to meet
Telepathy clairvoyance ready to greet
Sagely, delivering intuition
Wisdom from so long ago
Not to mention creativity
You will incontestably glow.

Greetings, salutations
Grand tidings to all
Atlantis is one too many
Don't contemplate or stall
Come through
Increase stride to masterfully collide
Clear all paths to thee
On three, one two three
Crystal clear— you see!

Solar
Tamed, of Ra, happy
Creative spark, that aligns
To soothe, to answer

Mommy's Teapot
    Sun kissed earth's mothering touch
    Captured essence natural flavor
    Herbs fruits leaves bagged
    Blended tradition seeped
    brewed for savoring thrill

    Soothing sip warming the inside
    Senses note feels and fills
    Knows so well inhales aroma
    All together sees steam
    Time traveling vapor

    From memories as words
    Floating in the mist
    Teasingly beg for a cup
    Swiftly dissolving mid air
    Lingering thoughts sentimental

    Reminiscence of mom
    A rose made with love
    Specifically for you

3

GROWING

EXPOSURE

*Evry day ah fishing day, but evry day
nuh fe catch fish*

ON THE EARS: Don't always catch fish
even on great fishing days

FOR THE HEART: Won't
always get accolades for actions
but consistency is nice.

For Give

For this Forgiveness ritual
Focus on the power of red
That cleansing
Purifying releasing red
Menses blood moon power
Letting go of what
No longer has any purpose

We will undress with
Elevated consciousness
Any person thing or event
Might even be we ourselves
Something internal
Whatever whomever
Caused us to hurt

Come along with me
Yes I
Relax any stiffness
You might be feeling in the body
Re—lax, relax
Eyes open or closed
You choose
Taking deep breaths
To activate awareness
To the rhythm of my voice, breathe
Breathe in—breathe out

With breathes identify
That person or event
Breathe in—breathe out
Breathe in—breathe out
Breathe in—breathe out

Now with third eye
Mind's eye
See a candle
A strong bright
Red candle
Breathe—breathe

I forgive myself
And those that caused pain for me
I forgive myself
And those that caused pain for me
As you breathe
Breathe in the affirmation
On exhale release, forgive
Visualize the candle melting

I receive forgiveness
And thrive from light and love
I receive forgiveness
And thrive from light and love
Visualize the candle melting
I cleanse anger from my life
In my mind and body
I cleanse anger from my life
In my mind and body

I choose love
I choose forgiveness
I choose love
I choose forgiveness
Visualize

Power to forgive myself
And others engulfs me
Power to forgive myself
And others engulfs me
Breathe—
When you feel ready
Slowly be present
In right here, right now

Breathe

So ova here waiting sitting humming
Cause this not easy
RASS no not at all
Might as well get one that's handy
Might not think it dandy but check it!

Been ova here steaming
Pressure that's been mounting
Ease just playing and playing
Pl—ay–in with these toys
Beginning to feel robotic even idiotic
Playing with only self

If joy comes in the morning
Why it can't stay the night?
Pure delight would have ova here
Constant moves on the merry go round
That's no good puts in a tizzy
Breeding ground feeding frenzy

Ova here taking head trips
Dream thinking
Why can't just do the love bumper boats?
You in yours and me in mine
Bumping into each other's— on purpose
Where G marks the spot
Never to cause hurt but just a tad of a jerk!
Harder if we like
All in the name of pleasure bare fun!

Breathing ova here
Believing in what I know
I know that God is good all the time and
All the time God is good
I know you are wanted by many
Connected to a few

I know the message you composed
Is important cannot be slowed
I know JAH is love and love is JAH
So inhale JAH exhale Rasta for I
Jah Rastafari

Well ova here feeling courageous
Confessing chanting it loud
If you love it set it free
It will come back if meant to be
Right there waiting that time
To simply breathe be

Lost
See that there
Is a new rave
Instead of
Hide n seek, now
There are
Hide n peek
It's no skin
Off the back
If someone loses
Lost everything already
Found peace
Hiding in self

No Puppet
What wants to see?
Worth known
Why can't just let ?
Just be?

Mus wear hair certain way
Cause it infuriates compelled
To always stare
Really stare

Mus dress
Conceal all fine
Curves and rise
Cause inside envies divine

Mahogany hue
That doesn't deceive
Catch looks in awe
Refuse believe
Can't believe

Mus act
Some kinda way
Not too loud
Don't say too much
Only when allowed
Better not touch

Moving strings
Like a puppet but
Only when says
Go now on show for show

Mus be
Figurine planted
Motionless while moving senseless
As pleased

Conspiracy smells
Costumed façade of coordination
Smarty pants or panties
You've been schooled
Unmistakably schooled

Ain't no sunshine when gone
Don't mistake
Confuse calculated captions
For some bourgeois bullshit

When it drops know it's
Spicy scotchy hot
Sizzling hot
Let's break it down
When getting ready over here
Out to somewhere over there

Making mellow tunes
Mind escapades to anywhere
Dare to hear come little closer
Over the shoulder right there
Sings already been there
Been there

Home
Where the hell am I?
How inna da world?
Gonna have to
What is happening inna my head
Not to mention inna my heart

Mind blindfolded face
Without a rass clue
Propelled to this state
Mostly eyes did dark
As that awful loop
Of remembrance replayed
And replayed and re—played
Seeing only mind instead

Recall asking, "are you scared?"
"Sometimes do, Nichie boo"
Throat died tight grasp of response
On full from pain said
"Always remember ova here scared"
"Feeling helpless too for u"

Replays are exhausting
Savage without any care
Choking poking
Squeezing breath outta voice
Pointless cover to plug ears
Constant devilish whisper
Thoughts with tears
Must get this shit out ahead!

Triumphantly
Courageously looked back
Confident ten years
Would lack any attack
From guilt or regret
This space this time and place
Holds distressing lot

It's a shot scored
To remember to not fail to recall
It's a shot through the heart
To relive plot holding it all
Land of birth absent one
Passage inna this earth

Tiny giant island
So love yet don't love you
Hate how much love
Haves for you
You are a magical place
Have identical her face
You are upbringing
She is beginning

Combing locations memories that roam
Protected treasures as she is home
Handling comfortably
Never to tell true discomfort
Pretending like not pretending

Presence engulfs
In everything there
Beauty incomplete
Without her it's bare
Voice touch motherly advice
Missing too lack of choice
To get them here
There anywhere

Wretched filthy heartless relentless
Mother-killing carcinoma
Left only traces just her aroma!
Anger has a scary face
So doe's pain
Sorrow has a real face
Lasting memories
Have many faces too

Just In Case
    If ever doubt cuts through the mind
    Trying to enter the heart
    Hitch a reverse
    Look to the very start

    How endured
    Held on did not depart
    Despite no word
    One other's part

    If ever fear
    Infiltrates the psyche
    Intending takeover
    Of the heart
    Remember to remember
    Look to the very start

    How didn't
    Jump to believe
    Lies fed to deceive
    But instead took
    Brave heart chance
    For truth reprieve

Learn to Live
Give gratefully,
Out of wealth to
Give

Accept graciously,
Out of knowing not
Coerced

Praise exultingly,
Out of glorification for the
Highest

Love recklessly,
Out of a joyful heart without
Fear

Learn devotedly,
Out of an insatiable appetite for
Knowledge

Dream unboundedly,
Out of believing the
Unimaginable

Live harmoniously,
Out of holding positive immune to
Negativity

Experience abundantly,
Out of openness all things are
Welcome
Learn to live live to learn

Now What

Why did this all happen
And when did it begin
Not thinking
Just sank so deep
Fell right on within

Total bliss and happiness
Sings the heart for him
Truly can't decipher
That moment head did spin
Never a feeling so heavenly
Completely under skin
Growing greater
for sure therein

Oh Wow!
    Stand here and sigh
    With needles as thoughts
    Sticking into the brain
    Painful effects down in the heart

    Gazing in awe
    What is twisted round?
    Waves of plastic lies tied to plastic smiles
    Probing considerations for what is perceived
    Ocean of pretense fishing to deceive
    Paper words hit
    That have no grit
    Such never stick but
    Flutter with slightest lift

    See movements
    Avenues of self-possessed
    Profiles fictitious stories
    Truths never expressed
    In a webbed trance
    Desperate measures enhance

Perfect image to uphold
For others to behold
Fame in success
Numbers hold all the gold
Basic two to witness
To narrate how stories told

Stay
Yesterday's spell was cast
Then only for farewell
It leaves so don't dwell

Tomorrow has its charm
Don't think too much
Sounding any alarm

Forget about what's to come
Just stay here with now
And succumb

Up in Smoke
Transformed
This eye, am I two?
A spanking new view
Has come through

Late for you
To drop, tuck
Cover or roll

Burned scorched
Filled with smoke
Your soul

Angel Card

> Is it necessary?
> To always shine
> Even the sun shows us
> Its back for awhile
> Allowing moonshine
>
> Must we always?
> Have strength to carry on
> What can haul the load drudge
> Constant to never ending
>
> Is it possible?
> To see time in abundance
> What race can run at full
> Throttle relentless to infinity
> Must all engagements?
> Include might and must
>
> Do you give?
> Everything and anything
> 100% each and every time
> Is it fact?
> That one can be jack of all trades
> Why does failure
> Always have to be the start
> Of a new start a do over

Do we ?
Need be punctual for life
Without fail or excuse
Ever never and always
If chasing such as these
Is same as hunting

Finding gold's pot at rainbow's end
Show up with best expecting success
Even failure count it as yes
For pursuing a perfect score perfectly
Is fleeting and losing the mind is insanity

4

EXPERIENCE

In Purpose
    Shackled by insecure
    Failed its done
    There is no more
    Frozen rigid sore loser
    Race not run
    Rat race cat race, race
    It don't matter
    Any face still last place

    Drag around blindly
    Don't even see it
    Using disappointment
    Defeat as a cane
    That guides steps
    Depletes all complete

Fix up slingshot
Aim and release
Shake that crippling
Hostage thinking beast
Power in purpose obedience trust
His will priority absolute must
Lead in conviction kingdom message sent
Father above said what he meant

The Address
    The uncertain
    Is where opportunity resides
    Cautiously yank it
    The unexpected
    Is where steam floats free
    Bring the fire to boiling
    The faithful
    Is where visions live this lifetime

    At the depth of joy
    You'll find gratitude
    At the heart of it
    Loyalty's muse
    At no end longevity
    Endure balancing portions
    For the *DreamKeypr's* box
    Nestled within the soul

Time Travel

Without realizing the hour comes
They lose all their power
By the time you note or notice
Neglect unravels it
Easy as counting ABC's
Memories wither away in a breeze.

From a quick turn aside
Interest unremembered
You're left with only pride
In the blink of an eye
Doubt spirals out of control.

With a tinge of delay, all the time
In the world can kangaroo
From surplus to deficit
Before you know it selections to choose
Transform to you snooze you lose.

Ruminating on the divine
Exemplars of experience
Shall we cease from over thinking
Over watching over, over-standing
Replaying silhouettes of slip ups

Shall we show loves we care?
Enter and be there
Speak their love language
Even if only for a moment.

Shall we not be paralyzed from fear?
Fear to speak, to feel to leave
To ride along to breathe
Shall we enunciate time?
In our endeavors.

As the tea loses steam
Days run away to months
That age to years
As sunshine switches places
With moonshine and clothes don't fit
They get shorter, not tighter.

Shall we not hesitate?
Too much procrastinate
As priorities change
Opportunities pass
Promises lapse, shall we not!
As good health leaves us
Ailments engulf us.

As toddlers turn to teens
Adolescents add up to adults
As parents impersonate their children
Till the very end
Shall we not wait until?
"I made it too late" is our song of sorrow.

Besties
How mi can say
What's best to begin?
To describe fantastic
Experience yuh bring
Some fi a reason
Some a season
Some can be fi learn a lesson

Fluid life list
Changing wid the tide
Ole names fall off
New names jump on
Mus Neva force
Fi stay on too long

Some names wid pleasure
Dem tag along
In good in bad
Fa betta fa worse
Dem do not depart
Closely dem follow
From the very start

Dis name type adds
Does not subtract
A plus always
Fa dem wid you
Vice versa plus fa you

Arguing and fighting
Sometimes mus
Better not intervene
Pick a side between trusts!
Both will jump
Shredding defense to dust

Adventure more exciting
Knowing cheers from you
Victory so much sweeter
Knowing can celebrate with you
Sorrow so much easier
Knowing can cry to you

The Unveil
Mask off mask on many in a lifetime we put on
Playfully deceiving a game of hide without seek
Concealing yet creating elusive hopes and dreams
Masks that tease, that grant, that please

Great care and caution should you wear them upon
As truth in self could shrink from strong
Stealthily it conforms its purpose to deceive;
Resisting might result in a tight, tight squeeze
Masks sometimes red maybe even blue
Haphazardly change meeting where what when why who

Security they give us familiarity we breathe
Broken or cracked destinations we consider bleak
Desperate and erratic are our feelings when one breaks
Compulsion to repair no solace freedom takes
A glance a reflection cannot see through
Ponder what happened not finding any clue

Despair taunts and laughs
Difficulty admits
The mask enveloped
Too good of a fit

Nowadays

Nowadays is obsolete
Tumultuous trumpets bellowing
For a grand announcement
Harmonious harps reverberating
Skillfully with a sly smile
Keenly listen for
Smooth rhythmic beats
Driving drums determined
To deliver a message
Nowadays is obsolete

Many cannot hear
Suspended they lag
Linger in pause
Refusing, refuting
Even rejecting
Answers expecting

Will you dare to look laboriously?
Will you care to listen attentively?
Are you ignorant so unaware?
From which we came?
Gizmos and gadgets
Already in our grasp

We are our need to procreate
Revivify possibilities beyond
Our wildest dreams
Starting first in self
That only one
Nowadays is obsolete

Hear the echoes of guidance
As Goddess whispers
Attune to Earth's grandiose power
She commands with the elements
Dance with the fluidity of water
The agility of wind
Confidently stretch from roots
Of her grounding
Yonifest greatness with
Transforming power of fire
Nowadays is obsolete

Hear the echoes of guidance
As God whispers
Attune to Earth's grandiose power
He commands with the elements
Dance with the fluidity of water
The agility of wind
Confidently stretch from roots
Of his grounding
Manifest greatness with
Transforming power of fire
Nowadays–
Nowadays–
It is obsolete!

Should

Is this true or a mystery
Should check for sincerity?
Is this hot or is it cold?
Should it matter if it tastes like gold?
Want it now or never?
Should say wants however?
Consider all could as yet?

Should care or get upset?
Can happy be here with now?
Feel better, but how?
Awake, yet still sleeping
Restless answers waiting
Should wrestling with could
Will surpassing might

Dirty "D"

Dirty & Disgusting
Always wanting
To disrupt
Invading sacred spaces
Never thought
To give up

Diligent & Determined
No preference slow or strong
With no care for who's here
There or wasn't wrong

Dangerous & Deadly
Infected affects left behind
Get away you dirty "D"
Blind, not blind
Can see!

Fast Talking
Slow down slow down what u chasin?
You keep racin intoxicated wid senseless
Sonny Boy it's not amazin
All this blazin just wastin
Your genius denseness leaves helpless
Is this endless?
Misunderstood sequence of events told
With destination as champion
You give glory you give praise
And fa poor journey there isn't any gold
You just scold

Scurrying like a squirrel without making a single note
Gave you the lesson plan you took it fa a joke
Slow down slow down what u chasin?
Dream shine you shine
Impress shine or moonshine
Your history was this
Not crawling first walking
Now running from pillow to post
Not a pot to piss in
Spending all the time
Doing nothing with everything
Leaving all sense behind

Did you sign up to use the head band?
Of the foolishness symphony
Listen up everybody knows
The blood type of failure is B negative
The type for success is always A positive
However success needs action and not a bag a mout

So set up get up ready up yuhself to win
Slow down slow down is what u chasin?
You never know that you the PRIZE
Thought you knew every ting all things me tings
You tings those things every single ting

Catch this advice and then mi done
Know who is at your table covering yuh six
Snatch the counsel of your dream team
Keep them in yuh midst
Think back to look back pon those wisdom talks
Seek a platinum piece for the platinum puzzle
Don't desist!
Not all mistakes can be corrected
Some can't resist

S L O W down S L O W down
No more running with neva see come see
You impressed too easily; it's not be frightened Friday!
Impatience derails the vision clearly
Up top, on top be grounded on these words
From the very beginning till must come ends
Fore experience jolt reality that you can't mend
Loving on you can't done
True word no pun

Power of Mind's Choice
    Yet to learn mindful control
    Thoughts fast or slow
    Heavy or light
    Equal still propels move
    No cares softens the blow

    Adjust smooth
    Positively lighten load
    Preventing negative ripple effects
    Affecting mindsets
    Echoing on and on and on

Letters

Gonna tell it on the tabletop shouting discrete
Gonna tell it underneath big mouth
Gonna tell it whispers sweet!
Loving on the alphabet
Just cause words are the language of love
Use them at work in play
Continuously whatever to say

It's really letters that win
Letters make words that cursive up
Making a sentence a phrase
A verse that runs off
Creating offspring in poems and paragraphs

That flourish and grow
That essays and memos note
That blossom to writings
That filter out to journals
That novels books

Dreamscape
Dream supreme excellence of creativity
Perfect in reality
Dream and know that thoughts are things
From a mind for it to make with it
Dream catchers invoke blinders front center
Tap that inner core
Dream for the Divine plan in Divine time
Steps along grit striding with fearless, flawless
Dream chaser, strap on success
Buckle up determination
Dream on dominion, never dominance
Confidence, potent boss power, limitless
Dream glazed full joy, all is restored
In absolute beauty
Dream savor dazzle, on purpose with purpose
Black pearl you plenty good thing
Dream speaking truth resolute no waivers
Beyond measure, trust
Dream keeper crossing seas of sacrifice
Manifest all which ancestors foretold

About The Trod
Up in the mountains
passing through valleys

———————

5

YARDIE VIBEZ

SHUTTER

Evry day devil help tief one day God
wi help watch

ON THE EARS: Every day the devil aids the thief;
one day Jah will help who's watching.

FOR THE HEART: The creator does not
sleep he rewards efforts of the righteous.

Yardie Cart

Broomie! Broomie!
Come get your broom
Step up pull up and come up
Long broom short broom
Healthy body broom
Nice petite broom
Yard broom house broom
Even cobweb brooms

Broomie! Broomie!
All colors over here
Black obsidian onyx, chocolate
You name it ebony charcoal melanin
Whole heap list steep
The handle have red
You see it dread
Gold look and behold!
Green for the message
Must be seen

Broomie! Broomie!
Come through pass through
Heed the verses from I and I
Sweep out all passa passa
Hatred sickness disease ill will
Envy fear violence
Mistrust distrust
Lies hurt deception
Addiction, depression anxiety
Sweep out all type of stress
You stress new stress distress

Broomie! Broomie!
Come get your broom
Greetings Empress
Long one? Short one?
Healthy body
Or nice and petite?
Which one? This one?
Give thanks!

Upful Energy
Hold a vibe on this ride
Pull up come up build up
Only positivity bless up!
Yes I
Boot up with positive visions

Power up on this electric ride
Positive energy glide
Straight from top full
To cheerful down to joyful
Strictly, surely no scourges allowed
All rough neck must slow and check
Before they end up in a wreck
Yes I

No ruffians in this crowd
JAH JAH know
Nothing but love
For every single one and one
All massive
Massive—all—for- love
Wheel and come again, back it up!
Love—for—all- massive
JAH love in constant motion
Yes I

Love all aboard
No room for worry
Never hold on tight
Relax revel in this
Moving meditation
Lifting you in flight

Elevated energy mindscape
Utterly out of sight
What type of?
Something is this
Irie energy vibe
Yes I
An overfull
Grand energy ride
Yes I

Yardie Roots
    Be still and feel it
    It's a divine natural mystic
    Omnipotent and everlasting
    It's in the soulful sensations
    Lifting you higher
    Beyond anything greater

    It's a meditation
    On purpose with purpose
    That spiritual connection
    Its pulsing vibrations
    From I and I to thee

    Can you hear– it?
    In praises exultation
    To the highest Jah Jah!
    In the royal teachings
    Lessons that guide
    Cosmic consciousness

    In eclectic music
    Enchanting powers within
    To roar, to begin
    In the devoted chatter
    Infectious laughter
    A movement for return
    From which we came

Tell me-- you see it?
On that universal anthem
Permeating
A perfect– heart– of love
On contented smiling faces
Absolute beauty
Beyond generational yearning

On blossoms of creative expression
Born from truth and history
On the promise of homeland
Majestic red green and gold

JJ Girl

JJ Girl, tie head or locks in –stead
Employing engaging enchanting
Menagerie of the whole lot
Epitome of creativity
imagination entwined in a melanin crown
Shining beacon that star you are
From that gallantry Garvey oeuvre

Fused majestic visions that inspire propel
Transcending time space place oh so well
Anchored in confident beauty municipal piety
Conceived from talks with freedom love and soul
Followed up with guidance walks, hikes or a stroll

Majestic wisdom from history vividly seen
Knowledge imparted from that of the queen
The epic legend our Nanny
JJ girl, sun-kissed island daughter
Imprints of your stride details left behind
Tales of glorious escapades-- splendor aligned

Memories that engulf tranquil peace and love
Blue lagoon and blue hole
Clearly places with much to be told
Picturesque fountains in nature
You show your presence there
Roaming about Somerset
With little time left to spare

A hop with a skip to reach YS Falls
For Black River's secrets
To share all in all
JJ girl, sweet hibiscus and vivacious
An incandescent performance
From your ebony zone
Glaring with healing powers
As an obsidian stone

You're green with promising trinkets
For all to partake and come get
Movements with agility
Elegance and grace
Exquisite hummingbird's flight
Hovering in place
JJ girl, true golden stroke
That tiny giant island evoked

Nice Up

    Ah so mi gwan when mi nice
    Make a sound sweet sweet sound
    Beat the dutchie pot covers
    On even the ground
    Gyrations jubilations for queens
    In track speed
    Victorious one two three
    Island girl power!

    Anytime is wine time
    Yuh ready there sister girl?
    Let's get it!
    Sip one, sip two, sip it smoothly
    All the way thru
    Ah so wi gwan when wi nice

    Ah so him gwan when him nice
    Bro and the banana tree
    Limb paid the price
    Lead foot was dangling
    Follow foot was piloting
    Should've known better
    Than all that gambling

Rasta man dey yah
Message true showstopper
When macka jook dem proppa
Them call fi dem momma!
Ah so him gwan when him nice

Ah so she gwan when she nice
Hot hairstyle no want it mismatch
Haffi draw fi the ghetto scratch
Cock head to the side
All four together it's Tap! Tap! Tap!

Happiness Station perfect destination
Joy controls the culmination
Ah so it gwan when it nice
Mantra as vow mantra for now
Full time every time all time

Ah so gwan when nice
Cool evening breeze
Lovingly under poinciana trees
Blossoms a cushioned sled
To lay blissfully covered
With care-free bedspread

What you say? you have di stool
Word stool power stool
Ah so chat when nice
The yard di yard
Nothing sweet like yard
Ah yah so nice!

Reggae Love
Every time we meet
real live exciting treat
    You greet wid a tickle pon the ears
    so much amusement it scares away the fears
        Ah long, long time mi love you
        love you love you, love you bad, bad

    To pick my spirit up, for you a simple feat
    Possess and charm never causing harm
spell bound to rub ah dub, bubble and
sometimes whine, not drink, but move round
the waistline

        Ah long, long time mi love you
        love you love you, love you bad, bad
          From days of ska and mash potato
          wheel and butta when music holds ya
Not to mention when feel a vibe
and bust out wid some skankin
or thankin a rent a tile partner
real top rankin

        Mi say, ah long, long time mi love you
        love you love you, love you bad, bad
          New name dance moves easily proves
          How power grows wider improves

More and more people getting in groove
with none a dem who disapproves
With ones butterfly gully creeper
wacky dip and willy bounce
make party sweeter
Mi can't even tell you
just how much mi love you
Ah long, long time mi love you
love you love you, love you bad, bad

Reggae Recipe
    Eh there selector up inna di dance
    Mi need the good good music
    so mi can bubble every chance
    every chance

    The making of a musical treat
    Feast for the eyes
    From tricks with a beat
    of limbs on a melody ride
    with a yardie vibe

    Ingredients easy to access
    that's tagged for a deal
    Jah know star
    You'll think it's a steal
    Get ready with the base
    Push in likkle treble

    Couple pinches of the chord
    an essential pitch reward
    A splash of sound power verses
    and bars that don't ever miss

Eh there selector up inna di dance
Mi need the good good music
so mi can bubble every chance
every chance

Blend the ingredients
mix out all the hiccups
When the time is set
Temperature all the way tun up
Emerging reggae evolution
Yes Iyah! That's what's up

Your body might consider
a slight tiny jiggle
but most definitely will sway
riding the rid dim music underway

Eh there selector up inna di dance
Mi need the good good music
so mi can bubble every chance
every chance

Reggae is sly
has a sneaky effect
Tickles of pleasure
you can surely expect
That falls upon the ears
it won't ever reject

Then before you notice
and beyond your control
It skips over your heart
prances on your soul

Every DJ betta know the reggae recipe
That island delight an eternal remedy
Reggae music mi say
you know it haffi sweet
Pure niceness you seeit

Jah Song

For Jah oh Jah
In love with love
On purpose
With purpose
In trust so trust

Do anything
With anything
Back then only then
Over time sometime
For them only them

With hope in hope
From now in now
For truth Jah's truth
So real for real

In greatness
With greatness
By faith in faith
Live life love life
With joy full joy
By Jah oh Jah

Live
Be
A vessel
Of Jah, pouring love sweetened
with inspiration mixed in Glowing
greatness in gratitude Intricate humility
woven within, harmony with self
Is balanced harmony
universally

RAS TAFARI

Head
distinguished one
in witness that must be revered
Awestruck,
that dynastic banner
with gladness you hold

Admiration,
vital lifestyle feeding
mind body and soul
Commendation,
red shield of valor
for the fallen forever with honor

Standing ovation,
golden triumphant hope
draped in courageous peace
Adoration,
ear-witness praise song
sincere and true
Jahrastafari!
ever living
faithful and true

Striving

Commander of the cosmos, creator
Majestic maker of our days
One enters into your presence
With thanksgiving and praise
Unwavering in your mercy
Grace you provide from above
Enliven I and I spirit with your perfect love

Lord of lords and King of Kings
Jah the high ruler
I and I timely provider
Master controller
Absolute in your power
Providing it is your will
Enlighten I with endurance
Patient traits to instill

Never to falsify accusingly
But testify devotedly
To exemplify beautifully
And to shine infectiously
Unwavering
With the essence of thee
For ones and ones to see

With sureness on your promise
Abundance for I and I to live
Knowing it's already been granted
These lamentations of I heart presented
Ase, amen and so it is
Amen, ase and so it is

Whatsoever things are true?
Whatsoever things are honest?
Whatsoever things are just?
Whatsoever things are pure?
Whatsoever things are lovely?
Whatsoever things are of good rapport?
Think on these things

Whose Mission

Come Bobo come Twelve Tribe
Carry unnu house and come
Binghy drum ah spit sound power
The place soon drop ah ground
Leggo all fear make haste
We haffi stand front center right there
To note and notice the scene
harken moves for what we glean

Tell elders they can't stand behind
Their role was predefined
As a matter of fact
dem need to guide the pack
cause all of us under attack.

No need for confusion or frustration
A revolution is not an illusion or
right this second solution. instead
Constant moving building
Evolving legacy
Resolution!

Let's take a moment of repetition
for the word le-ga-cy!--
Forfeit selfish focus of pride
Super ego visions that
stride with insides not holding
foremost yute's needs in sight.

Building a foundation on what's
really real what they can touch
see and be.
Not just concepts for a time in a while
that awakens spirits reimagine cares
Vibrating deep– but only on the ears
Rather, still and all something planted

Something planted seeds to take root
Sprouting to bloom and bear fruit
Something they can chew!--- on
Ingest digest deep down believe
strive and conceive.

King Selassie's teachings never lessons
of hate but peace and love
Lessons to cooperate to integrate!
The mission's value is far greater than
that of the individual impact
even for the visionaries

The majesty's message to prevent us
lest we fall too hard—
Peace demands the united efforts of us all
His imperial majesty Emperor Haile Selassie I
Kings of Kings, Lords of Lords
Conquering lion of the Tribe of Judah
Elect of God
Defender of the faith
The root of David

Ascension Key
   A paper light touch
   Gently to lips
   Exhilarating mind
   Anticipating distances
   As this encounter greets
   All things are welcome

   Senses healing
   No longer captive
   Sweet joy from aroma
   That does well to compel
   Propel no time to stay with play
   Tarry nor delay but
   Meditate journey up elevate
   Might even levitate

   Burning arms that reach
   To taste satisfy hungering
   Channel conduit supreme
   Spiritual disembodied connection
   To the highest
   Transforming green fire stick
   Smoke scent releasing visions sent

Premonition eyesight
Wealth of clairvoyant clarity
Clarity so rich so close
To hear sight ancestral teachings
Trust grounded in deeper faith
Hearing the sounds of what was
Sounds of what is
Sounds of what will be

One Love

Live by the spirit not
Please to gratify
Desires sinful nature
Discard don't pacify
Jah the perfect one
Non other could make man

Love on your brother
Lift each other live in peace
Not steering destruction aero
Causing it to cease
None return from whence
It comes controls
Light sound power stride

He saved us made all to live as one
No matter for race color where man from
Run from tempestuous wickedness
Greed arms up filthy deceit
Language spitting satan speech
Day of reckoning close within reach

Jah Love

O fear the lord you his saints
There is no want for those who fear him
Glory be to the father glory be to the son
Glory be to the spirit we desperately need right now
Glory be his light upon as he allows
The cross our might our savior
The cross our deadly ransom
O what a comforter
Universal creator

To him enter with good meditation
Rejecting Babylon them perilous situation
Refusing to be caught in any tribulation
Coming together with a love vibration
Yes I, people of every nation
In prayer look upon his face
Seek his word to find his grace
Your heart make him an abiding place
Belief in creator surest foundation
of any civilization–
Jahrastafari!

6

LIFE CHARMS

TEN

Can you imagine?
It is already TEN
Today is all about ten
1, 2, 3, 4, 5, are important
but 10 is TEN

Beautiful bouncy
Blue balloons, TEN
Napkins on the table, TEN
Ten candy crystals
In the candy bar, TEN
Candles on the cake
How many?
Of course, TEN

Giving you hearts and kisses
Most certainly TEN
Wishes to grant
I must aim for TEN
Digging for the treasure?
Keep looking to find TEN

Ten spectacular wishes
To commemorate TEN
Excitement with
Air of greatness
TEN! TEN! TEN!
Cocoa Princess is TEN!

Tighten Up!
Are you aware that none can compare
always a winner if you dared to show care
Increase your stride stay woke look alive
no door no window for you at the prize
Now is the time to frolic with might and
must, games of determined success and trust
On camera you excuse your face from the roll
even your voice you pretend a soul stole

Lace up with grit, stand tall, you're legit
Anchor down on respect, gratitude and grace
Without them in hand you won't have a place
Breathe in endless releasing possibilities
You, descendants' royal antiquity
Lineage of elders with unwavering dignity
Stolen and slaved for their brute strength
removing from power oppressors at length
Half-pint goliath island trend setting wealth
Everything plenty exceptional kid
Open wide all pride needed to build
Tighten up aim beyond the grid

TRY's Triumphant Answer
Drive actions starting
From patience compassion grace
Live lush and lovely

Brain visions likely
Heart captivates it lovely
Body speaks easily

Bell within ego
Conscience for peace harmony
Ring serenity

As We Gather

Circle without end
Cheers to honor celebrate
One love extends
Cause life begins at
Hearty promising bend
Gifting gratitude and heart
Pair of lovers to befriend

For travel on this journey
Sweet and savory blend
Keep them handy
Don't! never expend
Sum radical audacity no loose ends
Complete togetherness
Straight through to tail end

Love them stitch them together
Button them up!
Pin them to remember
Sprinkle some flower dust
Make 'em pretty
Make 'em plush
Weave 'em feel 'em
Hug 'em with a bow

Before you know it
Realizing the flow
Be celebrating milestones
Seasons of grow that glows

For things of beauty
Meant to be full joyed
Delicate things
Meant to be handled gently
Positive things
Meant to be secured
Joyful things meant to be kept
Lovely things are meant to be treasured

No Idiot

Enemy chases
For treasure you admit
No bae take a load off
Catch your breath for a bit
Enemies are better off
Need to just quit
Efforts scream time wasted
True misfit

Third eye sees deceit
Clear crystal
Real legit
Plans most certain to falter
Retreat they will commit
Unto conquering lion
With ease all submits

? I Am Who?
    Uncertain
    Envelopes all years
    Tucked tightly with happily sad
    Searching seeking for answers to find
    Yearning

    Alas
    Revelation dawn
    Has arrived with knowing and purpose
    Ancestors' shoulders on stands
    Proudly

Connected to the Cosmos
    Cosmically connected
    Celestial and escalated
    Enlarged extended elevated
    The cosmos have provided desideratum
    Vast possibilities any you can fathom
    Yet our performance is a crisscross
    on the contrary

    We retreat in our cocoon of humanness
    Humanness that finds comfort
    Sitting with fear that
    Cripples our mobility when
    Frightfully the fearful feeling is
    Ferociously greater than any
    Forbidding finish or end to contend

    We cloak our naked truth
    Masking to conceal our shame
    Shame that is in immortal combat
    With the mind, where victory is violent!
    Not as the mind dies but how—
    The fact that from shame's victory
    The mind devoured itself

You can discover your goddess view
Turn inward and scan intently
Your view you will see you
Your own self
Your unworldly espy
Perception in reality
Self-pace of affinity
Ultimate treasure the opportunity

Beauty In No Eyes
    Without eyes
    cannot see, the
    utter disgust they hate
    at thee
    Intuition speaks
    it's not that
    but with envy,
    jealous they attack
    Happy
    without any eyes
    to blemish, truth
    innocent beauty
    of mind

Alive

Determined to placidly float through
experiences seeking eye and caption splendor
To respond with colorful retort
that spins the argumentative into
senseless confusion

Persistent and poised
to execute while ushering out
Dismissing distractions
that lack substance and
are fine spun
from folly or tales

Audacious to step
to walk unknowing pathways
of dreams and visions
Firmly grounded
armed with strong values that
embody spirituality
A live feed to the divine

Selflessness thinking of others
in addition to self
Humility, inner sight
No need to be greater than
never feeling less than
Gratitude to live with
abundant appreciation

Finally to put love on display
To consent to love without hesitation
To plummet mindlessly in love

Cocoa Princess
Dazzling rich melanin
Soft coils in the air
Faced with plump lips
Curves with dips
Small rise for behind

Smooth island tan
Bronze-kissed skin gown
Radiance glistening
Straight from sole to crown
Lineage afro supreme excellence
Offspring generations of deligence

Decades of determination
Stamped in fore parents' genes
Blood line of ambition
Tenacity and grit
Maroon matriarch warriors
Never put aside or quit

Glowing with confidence
From under that crown
Crafted with intelligence
Calculated with care
Blessed with brilliance
Inheritance comes clear
Possibilities abound
Prideful she dares

Why Or Why

Head nah work right
It is so freaking temperamental
It broke out and run wild all ova the place
Mind nuh watch nuh face

It belly flops into a big hole of one type
of punctuation, the question mark
It does this on its own frequency and timing
Ah so it dweet, without the slightest warning
You eva hear people say bad things
happen to good people?

Why neva hardly eva know that a person
good til something bad happens
How come if you're soft spoken and quiet
it is confused for weakness?
If science made a way to read minds
Sure wouldn't have no friends and
wouldn't be di only one alone that
stop talkin to them

Why ever is there dissonance between
the mind and the vocal cords for some people?
Dem have a good talk but can't
walk wid it and do

Anybody know why attitude can't just crawl
up in bad feelings and wallow in it?
But instead have to do bad goodly

What in the world is the reason why?
mout say it love yet it does so bad
Why two plus three equals five
but a plus b is not ab
The real question is why the rass
school teach that and nobody use it

Why is the letter y a crooked letter?
Did it steal its form from v
Is what kind of juju following family?
why so many members die
Is jinx, jinx

Ok, this is a really good one
to seriously think about
Explain why some, repeating some
black people bleach dem skin while
some, some white people burn up dem self
in da sun for the darkest tan?

How is it love, if choice picks da one
that loves more and not
the one that true loves to have
a true relationship of love? –
It can't be love if choice neva pick
it can't be true if it's lying

Why is failure bent on making trying give up?
Cause the moment trying gives in
failure will be victorious
Back to love, why if love loves you
and you love love
love can't be enough?

Scratching head that principalities and power
feel they could wheel and turn
spin gig round first move there back ova here
ultimate destination to nowhere
and not think questions would ask? –
Them fool fool!
Why questions have to ask so much ?
Why– asking why

Just Like That

Just like that tables flip charts fly emotions taking a dive
Just like that turns upside down as pouts come round
Just like that thrown in deep surf or sink waves whole heap
Just like that growing pains without a parent holding reins
Just like that from youth to man with little direction
Just like that death stings tears run heart aches
Just like that holding memories to make them last

Just like that sneeze sniffles coughs hack and throats crackle
Just like that once was now is making changes improving
Just like that holding own mind strong in a good zone
Just like that life goes on to make better carry strong
Just like that words help conversations making sense
Just like that sibling touch so much love that says so much

Just like that peace again patting shoulders making friends
Just like that a shopping spree girly things cute as can be
Just like that bakes a cake pop up idea celebrates
Just like that oh gosh laughs out loud when smiles attack
Just like that after all paints the ceiling and doesn't stall
Just like that comes together backs feet make soup sweeter
Just like that this story ends soon another to start again

Watery

> Speech in tongues of gladness told
> Hold not worry feather light bold
> For all a wish to know this treasure
> To water respect and be kind
> for it's pure and real of any time
>
> Powers that are supernatural
> Aged with strength that is phenomenal
> A healing traveler it can be
> Window or door new eyes to see
> Change in perspective only wage or fee
>
> It feels heals
> It nourishes flourishes
> –It remembers–
> It cleanses
> It frees
>
> The eyes are bubbles
> Bubbles that travel from the heart
> When they burst they fall as tears
> Filled with love in every part
> These bubbles form as the heart
> Breathes in and exhales

A sigh that floats resting on face
Finding its sincere place
So when eyes see tears or
know dear that cries
Stay with awhile
Holding tender till waters dry

Water paradox of purity
Precursor creating opulent beauty
Quenching all facets
Along the thirst of life

7

AND SO IT GOES

ZOOM

No mug no bruk
no coffee nah dash wey
> **ON THE EARS**:
> The mug isn't broken therefore
> the coffee didn't spill.
> **FOR THE HEART**:
> Even in difficult times try to count blessings.

Deeply Rooted

He looms from above
Gaze frozen fierce
Baby brown blinkers
Burning broiling blistering hot
For its dirt!
Dirt that they throw at him on him

He tries
To hold back but can't
Water that overflows
His eye banks
For its dirt! even more dirt
That they throw

He recalls
This happened in the beginning
All through the mid-section and
Now even at the finale
For its dirt!
Dirt that they dash

He thinks
Rich maroon hue
From down underground
Some part sandy part clay
Maybe even gritty parts around
Can be found
For its dirt!

He knows its dirt
With tiny coarse pebbles
Can scratch or scar
If aim is bout right
It can go real far
For its dirt!

He listens
Rage yells discreetly
Inside his head as a flower lands
Gently, beauty to honor what's dead
For its dirt!
Dirt they toss

He is vexed
For beauty lands in dirt
To spawn
Beautiful grime beautiful smut
Beautiful crud beautiful muck
For its dirt!
Dirt they sling

He pats
His sun kissed cheeks
Moving a lock from the streak
Smile emerges as he knows
For its dirt!
Dirt that they fling
As they sing

But
He is a seed bury him!
It is dirt that will make him
GroW!

Black Is Beautiful
    Swift on some new programming
    Changing pronouns examining
    He she them or sometimes they
    Switching them vice versa
    Placing on display

    Adjusting religious beliefs
    From God Allah
    Experiencing the nirvana
    Altering what we eat
    As carnivores or herbivores
    Whichever being a treat
    A fancy or favor to make complete
    What about the new black outlook?

    Black is required for colors to have hue
    Black is beauty not dark or cruel
    The color black is powerful
    Vigorous real strong
    It soaks in all colors
    Reflects not even one

Black doesn't make
Magic scary or dreary
Wretched or dreaded
Black heart love's embedded
No part not symbol
Hate hurt or danger
So a blackheart man
Cannot hurt ya!

A blacklist
Tally of courage
Strength like this!
A black night
Darkness simply
Opposite of bright
Necessary to balance
Day with night

Stars shine more brightly
Against the darkest sky nightly
You are in the black
If performing well
Words like blackmail and black market
Now displaced!
Make haste warning others
Threat mail purchases at illicit market

Remember
Practice your black walk
Eradicate the previous bad talk
Black night brilliantly bright
A beautiful black heart
Inscribed with a blacknificent blacklist

The real black magic
Curating beauty
All wrapped in black
Sheer black sophistication
Feel the power of black
A new black outlook view
Bold black true

In the Know
Apprecilove
considerable power in words
Watch your mouth!
Realize
extraordinary power of thoughts
Charge, engage only positive energy!

Recognize
considerable power in association
See, to your friends it tells who you are!
Notice
supreme power in presence
Glance and then dance!

Phenomenal power
within phenomenally
Dare to believe dare to be

For The Bullies
Tried to destroy
As you see greatness
Sending love
To cushion fall
No imitating any part at all
Stop trying to follow
Doing all that extra stuff
Don't want it to hurt
Realize don't measure up

Putting pretentious disguise
Make up of outrageous lies
Isn't cloak hiding how agonize
Experiencing cognitive dissonance
From sight imbued radiance
Won't play with
Will pray for
All parts humble
All parts proud

Know Thyself
    Tan so back to watch the flex
    Y oh Y u think vexed
    Tongue as heavy as lead
    Most times live in the head
    Yes, walk n talk self very well
    Even answer get angry
    Sit sometimes dwell

    Muted soundless not stupid senseless
    Cause creation begins there timeless
    Love an ingredient in that make
    Exercise n give whether or not take
    Shine light show love shout it modest
    Comes from extras legit and honest

    Reciprocate or multiplier
    Would be a plus plus!
    But never a must must!
    As it takes willing water
    No fuss fuss!

Peek inside entirely
Heart drums vitality
Humbled truth beaming
Surrendered love overflowing
Agape majestic from above
Cascading upon to love
To me from me sincerely

Where

Pistachio ice cream.
Eagerly last saw you
brought it willingly.
Hopefully waiting promise
never fulfilled, fulfilled.

Where, where is the love?
You should have
Didn't have enough to share; spare.
Hear other children calling out
to theirs, tears.
Dreaming no wishing
could holler out for years, years.

Scattered puzzle pieces.
Missing more than a few, true.
No one to assist or
persist with any clues, clues.
Did ever wonder or
try to know, no.

Faded pages blinded with time.
Haystack digging within
for a needle, needle.
Rather try and try
with hope for something, anything.
Wanting peace of mind, mind.
Peace and truth, truth.
Because truth is love, love.

Natural Woman
    Within untamed woman is free
    Of her she is seen
    Engage her interest
    All will see
    Breathtaking fascinating
    Captivating will find her
    Intoxicated longing
    She'll make stir

    From gaze directed
    Fixated towards thee
    Responding with pledge key
    Spelt undeniably as promise
    No intention to flee

    To give unrestrained unrestricted
    Heart to process emitted
    For the stages
    Wholeheartedly committed
    Commits to a tantalizing dance
    Captivated in a trance

Embracing life with death romance
Prance of end angel's brush
Understanding in advance that it's
Never a game of chance but
A splendid circumstance

Tears are cleansing
Provides new window to see
Visions new lens 360 degrees
Pure nature calls on the
Power of the drum that hums
Beats to create to become

Mosaic of emotions entwined with desire
She's the epitome downpour of power
An awesome wonder many will admire
Conquering beauty transforming fire

Absolute certainty crystal clear clarity
Receipt of her ought to be swiftly
Fearfully rejecting not wanting to see
Refusing to be results
Untimely regrets most earnestly

Ra
With bated breath earth deliberates
In awed wonder it considers
Fullness of majestic power
With one half of face
That shines so bright
Illuminating visions
A source for delight
Onto the horizon even further on

Lady bountiful
Guardian that provides and energizes
With firm warning
To make all kinds aware
Never to stare or get too close
All the same to be—ware

As she turns
Staging to set her face
Within her own pace
Side two directly in view
To captivate with
Whispered hues of beauty
From silky soft strokes
In subtle small doses
She blankets the land
Lulls it with soothing cradle song

Ra—
Earth rejoice and be glad
For the plenty of her bounty
She gifts onto you
Ra—
And that includes
Loyalty demonstrated
Ra—
Each day
Again afresh renew
Ra—
Tomorrow the sun
Will shine through

Pantoum of June Blues

No end in sight hanging with this plight
The scar of death still lingers
Marked the heart from the start
Held on tight
rom a bite venom splinters

The scar of death still lingers
Thoughts replay day to day
What could've made her stay?
From a bite with venom splinters
Head contends and tries to mend
All erratic pieces

Thoughts replay day to day
What could've made her stay?
Words hide from see
 Look but cannot be
Head contends and tries to mend
All erratic pieces

Muted solace torments the soul
Has as its goal to never ever free
Words hide from see
Earnest look to make but cannot be
Destined for infinity–

The route to take on this flight
Muted solace torments the soul
Has as its goal to never ever free
No end, no end in sight
Hanging with this plight

Shining

Shine baby shine
Light's a treasure
Stay pon practice till cut straight
Laser focus eyes on solution prize

Never stay wid problem
Keeping front and center view
It will play all day
Tricking to sway
Away far and surely stay

Don't be discouraged
No retreat no surrender
Be courageous you're strong
Won't see you coming
All will be dead wrong

For its light no sound
Never rolling on the ground
Ignite!
There needs be light
To aid sight in the darkness
For it's light in the flame
Eyes for the vision

Need only make ultimate decision
Appears real dark but find a spark
Simply angle it doesn't seem bright
Approach situation keep things tight
Moving from try-angle
Proudly make stand up fight

Get real close be forthright
Ignite you're foresight
Shine it some light
Making it out of sight!

8

STILL DREAM

Renew
    Beauty in darkness
    Time for rest
    Rest for best
    Blankets the earth
    Completing the circle
    Bringing forth

    Opportunities renew
    Possibilities anew
    Another chance
    Another way
    New beginnings
    New day

Beacon still shines
There is daylight
Rest relaxes body and soul
Curating splendid dreams
The keepers behold

Don't You Know
    Lift your head up little lady
    All well with precious baby?
    Why such a frown?
    Grunt no word sound
    Sound as you speak
    Response to call
    Was passing salute
    No intention to stall

Now compelled
To gauge your spirit meter
For it bends and bows
An ugly frequency tweeter
Tweeter that screams
Don't you see? come support

    Without even asking
    Jump in don't abort
    Sight to push forth
    Memories relate and report

Don't you know you're a winner?
That one from a race
A race of live or die to create
Knitted together by the high creator
With gorgeous shades hues of black
Kinky curly medley
That doesn't lack

Don't you know?
The luring zeal
Snowflake obsidian appeal
Speckled with colors
Black with white
Equal happy together bright

Don't you know?
They are never more
Never less but right here
In midst of it
Same as you so
Never quit!

Don't you know?
History from which you came
Royalty tower you align
The daughter of freedom fighters
That shattered their shackles
So justice could stand here

Now you know
Glow as you grow
Cast your eyes above
Capture charm and splendor
In endeavors
Crown will come along

Emergence
When certain time has now come
Imagining orchestrating
Boundaries must succumb
Laying foundations
Unveiling grand master plan
Duty compels trust must can

Wondering no dear listening!
With royal ancestors to stand
Overflowing imagination
It's a hologram

Manifesting greatness in galactic program
Acknowledging the invisible
To create unimaginable
Ears witness eyes caption

Infinite Wisdom
    Infinite wisdom of the universe
    In your divine time
    We welcome serenity and accept
    Tickles with smiles when dejection
    Is an ambush to our
    Verses that speak and ease
    When sadness intrudes
    A smothering embrace for our spirit
    When it bows or sags
    Friendship that adds glitter days
    for days, in fact all days

    Infinite wisdom of the universe
    In your divine time
    We welcome serenity and accept
    Beauty to behold
    To encounter on life's trod
    Thru and thru
    Faith for mind's sight
    To trust to believe
    The courage to lean in
    To examine thyself
    Clothes of patience
    To cover naked truth

Infinite wisdom of the universe
In your divine time
We welcome serenity and accept
A Spirit of tenacity
When doubt fear confusion
Creeps stealthily in
Devoted daily devotion
That ends in time
With forever
Patience to practice
Peeling back layers
A reflective sincere endeavor

Infinite wisdom of the universe
In your divine time
We welcome serenity and accept
Boldness to move sway
Even jiggle it baby!
To rhythm of sweet happy
Third eye intuition
To decipher codes of the cosmos

A commitment
To sight of one that was
To revel in one that is!
A dream keeper's soul
ASE amen and so it is
ASE amen and so it is

Scorpio's New Moon

One zodiac new moon
A constellation's beaming bloom
New arrival in galactic commune
November plus four for fourth 2021
Equals eleven
Following numerology plan

Testifier to witness
Make haste it's nutritive
Grand master psychic intuitive
Turn east four hours
Past meridiem and quarter
Head over west a tad bit earlier
Making view even merrier

Look within
Feel the awakening
Internal antenna extending
Outstretched and peeking
Number one and one
Stretched tall bright
Gateway connecting
To divine delight

Power unleashed
From rhythm of drum
Away with coerced servitude
Ushering compassioned in-service
Cooperative and of service
Cosmic out of sight
Angles of two opposing
Clear standing in view
Moon that's new

One set at twelve degrees
The flip side agreed
Degrees twelve a guarantee
Perfect astrology scene
Creating eclipses to glean
Star codes of might pleasure upright
Champion freedom fearless outright

Assumptions all to value
Top-down approach from heaven inverted
Starting with self it converted
Tis new moon
Beginning to remember
Cleansing impulsive
To disencumber

Hiccups that impede
Won't let arms reach
Untangle cords of truth
Curious as in youth
With grounding culmination
Revolving grateful celebration
To enjoy abundant beauty
Pleasure of life to employ

Skin Cover Lover
Right here not see thru
Dark cover glows in view
It nuh fair fi compare
Neither scorn nor stare
Your cover can stay
So why must mine go?

See yours out and bright
Soaking up attention limelight
Love flows under cover
Same fi you and all every other
Beauty bundle brilliant black
Real black magic it's a fact

That Song

Can an intro to a song
pull you in so deep?
And without any effort
Compel you to leap
The words the chord
Make your heart smile
You trust enough
To get lost in it awhile
The rhythm the beat
Awakens your soul
Might this be part?
Your destiny's scroll

Cannot understand it
Need to believe in it
Complete joy
You feel with it
You want it
But then without warning
The music just stops
Your heart skips in beat
As you try to repeat

Your efforts are pointless
The song does not play
You sit and ponder
Whether you should stay
Cannot comprehend it
Need to believe in it
Should there be trust for it
That song, that song
You need it!

The Charm of A Woman
    No line crossed there's no line
    In front behind or beneath
    Please put away ova there
    For none's right here
    If hinders connecting with thee

    Boundaries kept high from wall
    Towering tall securing self
    That of refugee's call
    Jah sent through visions
    Mystical deal captivated propelled
    Practically compelled
    Steps into dream out clear view
    Right in front of you

    Humility and grace heart with one face
    Moving a steady pace
    Spreading love like a virus
    Shimmering beauty downright desirous
    Tethering steps moves that steer stride
    Heading on the opposite side
    Focus for to catch up
    Not embracing time to give up

Tormented from what truth feels
Enjoying emotions coming in real
Knowing full well ultimate love spelt
Where there's a woman
There is magic

It's alright its ok won't stop it must say
Doing that again
It's alright its ok won't stop it must say
Decided to free fall in love the other day
So will grow in love same way

Persevere
In endeavors be persistent poised
To execute while ushering out
Dismissing distractions
That lack substance
Fine spun from folly or tales
Just in time
When fear won't let go
Chew words to caress and show
Remind how much you glow

Dos and Don'ts
      The world has parts that are real ugly
      They spoil the shine of God's glory
      Let us stand his children
      Moving strong to fix
      Adding his love spirit perfect in the mix
      Don't lie don't steal don't fight or curse
      For those to God are the worse

      These don'ts are of the devil
      Oh boy! does he like to meddle
      Come together hold hands and try
      With all our might we'll make God smile
      Do truth do love do honesty and respect
      God will be happy
      I'm sure I bet

That's All It Took
The eyes did it, voicing its hello
Beamed through the thick
Deep into her essence
The inner woman anima stumbles
On presence, aura persona
Heart reflecting him

What Else

Pendulous motions through roles of living
Willing caring loving on occasion forgiving
Muted so long lost sight of face
A Mrs. Known yet unknown
Engulfed self-space

Equanimity offered splendid invite for treat
Tip toes past shadows determined to greet
Slight introductions first with tease
Imperfections allowed no judgments pleased
Imperturbable self-love spectacular embrace
No cares for masquerading with it has no place

Deep breath in fears doubt out
Faith confidence joy the only route
No movements from should
Heartily grounded proud
For the now begins
Dreams that live out loud